CRISIS COUNSELING IN THE CONGREGATION